W9-BCY-559

Discovering *ART*

Graphic Arts

Gail B. Stewart

ReferencePoint Press®

San Diego, CA

About the Author

Gail B. Stewart is an award-winning author of more than 250 books for children, teens, and young adults. She lives in Minneapolis with her husband and is the mother of three grown sons.

© 2015 ReferencePoint Press, Inc.
Printed in the United States

For more information, contact:
ReferencePoint Press, Inc.
PO Box 27779
San Diego, CA 92198
www.ReferencePointPress.com

LIBRARY OF CONGRESS CATALOGING-IN-PUBLICATION DATA

Stewart, Gail B. (Gail Barbara), 1949-
  Graphic arts / by Gail B. Stewart.
    pages cm. — (Discovering art)
  ISBN-13: 978-1-60152-698-4 (hardback : alk. paper)
  ISBN-10: 1-60152-698-9 (hardback : alk. paper)
  1. Commercial art--Juvenile literature. 2. Graphic arts--Juvenile literature. I. Title.
  NC997.S74 2014
  741.6—dc23
                                                                2014016054

Contents

The "Everywhere" Art

The image takes one by surprise. At first it seems to be merely a drawing of a jar of horseradish sauce with a spoon leaning against it, a scene so realistic it could be a photograph. But something about the drawing seems a little off—and then one realizes that the shape of the shadow does not match the jar's shape at all. In fact, the shadow cast by the spoon and jar is precisely the shape of a hand grenade. It is exactly at that moment that the message comes through loud and clear: This brand of horseradish sauce is strong—not for the faint of heart. And not a single word was needed.

An Effective Way of Communicating

This is an example of graphic art, a means of communication that has been around for thousands of years. From the early humans who left colorful cave art showing where the best hunting spots were to the knights who carried shields embellished with colors and symbols identifying their lineage and their place of origin, people have been using art, text, symbols, or a combination of these elements to deliver a message in an eye-catching, visually pleasing way that a verbal message cannot.

Unlike fine art such as painting or sculpture, which are created primarily for the purpose of self-expression, graphic art is a means of selling a product, motivating or persuading people to do something, or communicating something about oneself. For instance, when a new business opens, often one of the first decisions the owners make is to hire a graphic artist to create a logo that can be used on everything from business cards and stationery to the sign on the door. Fans of sports teams wear sweatshirts and caps emblazoned with team emblems designed by a graphic artist. A campaign button or a bumper sticker can show how one feels about a particular issue or announce the candidate one hopes will win in the coming election.

The Explosion of Graphic Art

In the twenty-first century, the use of graphic art has increased as never before. Whether paging through a magazine, shopping for groceries, or frequenting a favorite website, people are besieged by thousands of examples of graphic art each day. From the colorful packaging of cereal boxes and the layout of the morning newspaper to the easy-to-spot road signs warning drivers to merge with traffic, graphic art images are everywhere.

Graphic artists, also called graphic designers, frequently use both art and text to get their point across. However, in many cases the art alone can do the job. Traffic signs, for example, rely on an understood collection of symbols that can communicate important information to a driver. A red circle with a diagonal red line through it means "forbidden" or "no." The art within the circle communicates what it is that is forbidden—from a simple image of a campfire or cell phone to an arrow pointing right to indicate a right-hand turn.

Other well-recognized symbols include the colors of a traffic light, the six-pointed star of the Jewish faith, the cross as a symbol of a Christian church, the swastika symbol of the Nazis, and the peace symbol. In most public buildings a symbol on the door of a restroom indicates whether it is to be used by men or women.

The Role of Graphic Art

Most of today's graphic art reaches far beyond traffic signs and public restrooms. To create it, graphic artists rely on a variety of high-tech

Fans at a baseball game wear caps and shirts featuring team logos. Logos that symbolize sports teams, as well as other kinds of businesses, are created by graphic designers.

tools, some of which are computer applications. From the particular style of type to the size of the image or the colors, the designer must make dozens of decisions that will determine whether the graphic art is effective. Should the art be cartoonish or more serious? Should a photograph be used instead? Is text necessary, or can the art alone convey the intended message?

The specifics of the job depend on the audience and the message. Even so, the overarching aim of any type of graphic art must be clarity, or it will fail in its purpose. That purpose may be to communicate information about an upcoming concert or create an entertaining magazine ad for a new action movie. Its aim might be to make a brochure that will convince people to vote for a certain presidential candidate, or even an ad to convince a shopper to buy a particular brand of deodorant.

But no matter what the purpose of a specific design, the skill with which the designer creates the art or chooses the style of type to be used will have an immense effect on its success. Notes British designer Richard Hollis, "Designers, as well as the public, when asked for a definition of good design will answer, 'Does it do its job? Did message A get communicated to audience B?"[1]

Chapter One

The Foundations of Graphic Arts

Not until the late nineteenth century, known as the Victorian era, did the concept of graphic design become widely known in Western society. For the first-ever world's fair, known as the Great Exhibition of 1851, Queen Victoria and her husband, Prince Albert, invited the nations of the world to showcase the advances they had made in science, manufacturing, and technology. Many of these advances had to do with printing and the use of color and varieties of style for text, as well as the emergence of photography. More than 6 million visitors from around the world viewed these new technologies. It was clear then that graphic art was revolutionizing the way people communicated, sold things, and expressed themselves via a combination of art and text. However, for thousands of years, people all over the world had been making contributions to graphic art.

The Egyptians' Books of the Dead

Beginning around 1600 BCE, the ancient Egyptians used graphic art as a means of helping dead pharaohs navigate to their place in the afterlife. The Egyptians believed that when a person died, he or she was immediately in danger from terrifying monsters whose aim was to keep the dead from reaching the afterlife. Scribes and artists combined their talents to create maps complete with magic spells that would enable the dead to bypass the dangerous creatures residing in the underworld. The combinations of maps and text were known as Books of the Dead.

One image frequently seen in Books of the Dead was a hideous monster named Ammit, who was the judge and executioner of the underworld. Ammit was believed to eat the bodies of the dead who could not answer her questions correctly. Artists portrayed her with the head of a crocodile, the torso of a lion, and the hindquarters of an immense hippopotamus—the three animals the Egyptians deemed the most ferocious. Not surprisingly, the spells and diagrams pictured in the Books of the Dead that explained how to avoid Ammit and other perils were considered invaluable.

The earliest Books of the Dead were created long before paper was invented, so they were carved directly on the walls of a pharaoh's tomb—an expensive process. By 1475 BCE, however, the use of papyrus to make paper made it possible for everyday people to afford Books of the Dead, too.

Early Graphic Design in the Scriptorium

Centuries later, during the Middle Ages in Europe, beautiful examples of graphic art were created in the form of illuminated, or illustrated, manuscripts—almost always copies of the Bible or other religious documents. Though the printing press and paper were in use in China, both were unknown in Europe in medieval times. As a result, all manuscripts were copied by hand on calfskin, known as vellum.

Most of the manuscripts were produced by monks who worked in a large room known as a scriptorium within a monastery. They worked with quill pens made from the feather of a goose or crow. The ink they used was derived from plants, berries, burned wood, or minerals that could give them the colors they needed. The writing, known as calligraphy, was quite ornate, with designs and decorative marks that made the text more pleasing to the eye than plain text.

But copying the text was only part of the job. Frequently, a large, fancy capital letter would be highlighted in a rainbow of colors—from

> **Words in Context**
> *illuminated*
> A word that describes the first manuscripts that were decorated with hand-drawn illustrations.

This example of a medieval illuminated manuscript fancifully depicts Adam and Eve in the Garden of Eden. The text is written in the ornate script known as calligraphy and includes a large, elaborately decorated capital letter typical of such manuscripts.

deep blues and reds to glittering inks made from flakes of gold or silver mixed with a bit of egg to give them the right consistency. Each page also featured illustrations and border art.

No mistakes were allowed on these manuscripts. If a copier or artist made an error, the entire page had to be redone. Not surprisingly, a short manuscript might take six months to a year to complete, while a single copy of the Bible could take a team of monks working eighteen hours a day as long as ten years to finish.

Gutenberg's Contribution

Because of the intense, detailed work required to make books by hand, few people owned one. An individual possessing a Bible during the fourteenth and early fifteenth centuries was almost unheard of. In fact, many churches did not even have a copy. However, that changed drastically in the mid-1400s, thanks to a goldsmith from Mainz, Germany, named Johannes Gutenberg.

Gutenberg did not invent the printing press—printers in China had been using printing presses since the thirteenth century. Instead, Gutenberg's genius was in perfecting printing techniques, as well as realizing what could be accomplished by combining the printing press and movable type. Until that time, the early printers relied on wooden or clay blocks painstakingly carved with drawings or raised letters (in reverse). But the blocks were not durable; they tended to crack and split after just a few uses.

Gutenberg believed that movable type made of metal was the answer. He used an alloy, or combination of metals, including tin, lead, and a shiny gray mineral called antimony. The type he created was strong enough to be used over and over again. He also created an oil-based alternative to the water-based inks that printers used, which was less likely to smear or puddle during the printing process—especially when it came into contact with his metal type.

> **Words in Context**
> *vellum*
> Treated calfskin used in the Middle Ages as paper for handwritten documents.

Gutenberg's name is most often linked with the edition of the Bible he printed with movable type in 1454. Each page had forty-two lines of text and was printed at an astonishing rate of three hundred pages per day. Gutenberg left spaces for illustrations and highlighting that would be done by hand later. The Bibles were written in Latin and came in two-volume sets, each with six hundred pages. By 1500 half a million books had been printed throughout the cities of Europe on movable type printing presses using Gutenberg's system.

Moreover, not only were books becoming available to the masses, but so were calendars, posters, political pamphlets, and advertising leaflets. With so much demand for printed material, it is not surprising that there was a printing boom. By the time Gutenberg died in 1468, there were one thousand printers in Germany alone that were using Gutenberg's system.

The Rise of Literacy

The printing of the Gutenberg Bible occurred at the beginning of the Renaissance in Europe, a time when there was a new emphasis on literacy throughout all levels of society. At the same time, the arts were booming—writers of all kinds were producing poetry, plays, and novels.

One of the most interesting effects of Gutenberg's accomplishments was the rapid demand for reading material. As affordable books became increasingly available, more and more people were eager to buy them. By 1663, another exciting medium appeared, as the first magazine debuted in Germany, and within several decades other magazines were launched throughout Europe.

At first magazines had a target audience of very narrow groups of readers, such as scholars or people working in certain trades. But by the late nineteenth century, magazines aimed at the general public had emerged—including literary journals, sporting news, and magazines that included stories and poetry. And no matter what the content, magazines depended on graphic artists. Whether designing an attractive logo for the name of the magazine or creating an appealing cover and layout for stories and articles, these artists were key to luring readers to purchase magazines.

The Illustrated Cover

One of the most widely read magazines in the United States was the *Saturday Evening Post*, which debuted in 1897. The *Post* prided itself on having the most talented illustrators and graphic artists to design the covers of each edition of the magazine. The most famous of these was painter Norman Rockwell, hired at age twenty-two in 1916 by

Flanked by assistants, Johannes Gutenberg prints the first page of the Bible for which he became famous. Gutenberg's innovation of movable metal type revolutionized printing techniques.

Post editor George Horace Lorimer. Rockwell's realistic, colorful covers showed scenes of American life that resonated with readers.

Many readers admitted that it was Rockwell's art that drew them to subscribe to the magazine. "We had a subscription for years," says retired teacher Doris Lee Anderson. "I remember my kids wanting to see the new cover every time the magazine arrived in the mail. They'd look for the stenciled 'Norman Rockwell' in the corner. But I actually think they got pretty good at spotting a Rockwell cover even without seeing the signature. His style was just so unique."[2]

Many of Rockwell's covers were bittersweet, evoking nostalgia for childhood and simpler times, such as showing a girl apparently beating two boys at marbles or a 1923 cover with a little boy trying to nurse his sick dog back to health. Although the covers created by Rockwell and other illustrators were an important part of the magazine's appeal, Rockwell was modest about his work. "I showed the America I knew and observed to others who might not have noticed,"[3] he said.

Who Wrote the Devil's Bible?

The largest surviving illuminated manuscript from medieval times is known as the Codex Gigas, Latin for "giant book"—an appropriate name since it weighs more than 165 pounds (75 kg). Its pages were made from the skins of 160 donkeys. The manuscript comprises not only the Vulgate (written in Latin) Bible, but also many other historical documents in Latin that were said to contain all human knowledge at the time. The manuscript is often referred to as "the Devil's Bible" because of the large, strange illustration of a devil on page 90 of the book. The mystery of the Codex Gigas is who wrote it.

Experts believe the Codex Gigas was written in the thirteenth century in a Benedictine monastery in what is now the Czech Republic. But what puzzles them is that scientific tests sponsored by the National Geographic Society, including handwriting analysis, show without a doubt that the entire book was handwritten and illuminated by only one person—virtually impossible for such a monumental task. However, a famous legend that circulated centuries ago held that a monk had broken his vows and as punishment, the monastery walled him within a room to work for the rest of his life on the manuscript. According to the legend, the monk made a pact with the devil to help him finish the manuscript more quickly, and in return he included the drawing of the devil in the manuscript.

For fifty years Rockwell was one of the *Saturday Evening Post*'s most popular artists, creating more than three hundred covers during his career.

The Advent of Photography

While cover illustrations were big draws for magazines, the development of photography began a new chapter for graphic artists. A camera in the hands of a skilled and intuitive photographer could make a powerful statement unrivaled by any illustration. When entrepreneur Henry Luce founded *Life* magazine in 1937, he turned it into the first-ever photojournalism weekly, giving readers a close-up look at the world around them.

Some of the magazine's photos captured joyous occasions, such as the 1945 photo of a sailor kissing a nurse—total strangers—in Times Square upon hearing that World War II had ended. Others were ironic, such as one taken by world-renowned photographer Margaret Bourke-White in 1937 that showed a long line of people seeking food at a relief station in Kentucky after a massive flood of the Ohio River. The line stretches in front of a billboard showing an illustration of a happy family of four (including the family dog) riding in a new car. The billboard's message, contrasting with the line of hungry people, proclaimed in large letters, "World's Highest Standard of Living."[4]

Though *Life* was a pioneer in the use of photos in graphic art, other magazines began relying on photographs to boost their appeal to readers as well—a trend that has continued into the twenty-first century. One of the most talked about has been *Time* magazine's cover on March 17, 2014. It featured a panoramic view of New York City taken from the tip of the spire of the new One World Trade Center—the tallest building in the Western Hemisphere. The photo required the cover, last page, and two fold-out pages to show the result of 567 photos taken over a five-hour period. The magazine came up with the idea of shooting the photo because it wanted to "create a new image that would memorialize the rebirth, the healing of Lower Manhattan following 9/11," explains Jonathan Woods, *Time*'s photo editor. "More than anything, when people see this photo, I hope they appreciate being brought somewhere where they can't go."[5]

The Art of Type Fonts

In a work of graphic art, no matter how interesting the art is—whether an illustration or photograph—it is imperative that the type chosen for the text is attractive and easy to read. In the early days of movable type, the styles were limited. The type Gutenberg used was called Blackletter, sometimes known as Old English. It was based on the ornate calligraphy monks used in their manuscripts, with each letter made up of both bold and light lines, called strokes. An example of Blackletter used today is the type used in the mastheads of the *New York Times* and the *Los Angeles Times* newspapers.

But Blackletter had definite drawbacks. Because of the combination of bold and light lines, and because the letters had little space between them, a manuscript written completely in Blackletter could be difficult to read. To address the problem, printers and designers began coming up with new styles of type. Each style, or font, was different. Some fonts had letters that were angular, others rounded. Some featured "fat" letters, meant to call attention to a headline or advertisement, while others were designed to be easy on the reader's eye for long pages of text.

Another characteristic of a font style is whether or not it has serifs. Serifs are the tiny decorative strokes—sometimes known as tags—that appear on capital and lowercase letters in certain fonts. The bottom of a capital *A*, for instance, often has two serifs—small horizontal lines on the bottom of the letter's two lines. A font that does not use serifs is known as a sans serif (French for "without serif") style.

Influential proponents of sans serif styles included a group of German designers who, from a design school known as the Bauhaus that was open from 1919 to 1933, introduced a variety of creative designs for items ranging from architecture and furniture to type. Bauhaus designers rejected the ornate type styles so common in the Victorian era as overly fussy, preferring instead the simple lines of sans serif fonts. "The idea was that sans serif type was cleaner, less cluttered, and way more modern," says retired printer Don Berg. "If a company way back then wanted to show that it was more current, more up-to-date, their brochures were done with sans serif fonts—it was the way to go."[6]

> **Words in Context**
> *serifs*
> In certain fonts, small, decorative lines on letters of the alphabet.

The Messages of Type

In the years since Gutenberg lived, more than one hundred thousand styles of fonts have been developed, ranging from very decorative to very plain. Today graphic artists depend as much on type style as they do on the images they create for items such as posters, magazine ads, or book covers. As font choices have expanded dramatically, so too has the role of type.

Over the years, type has become an artistic element—not simply the letters that form the words of the text. As design educator Robin Landa notes, "Used in conjunction with a visual, type is often the verbal part of the design message. However, type can also be the visual itself and can express the entire message."[7]

Sometimes that message is enhanced by the way the type is physically spaced. For example, one clever use of type spacing appeared in an advertisement for GEICO auto insurance. The art is a photograph of a driver in a car with a crumpled bumper. The headline reads, "If you think seat belts will wrinkle your outfit, imagine what your dashboard will do to it."[8] But what is far more eye-catching are the three paragraphs of text underneath the headline—due not to what they

Although printing today is most often created with computerized fonts, for hundreds of years printers used metal type like that shown here to form words and phrases for printed materials.

The Graphic Art of Harry Potter

Some of the most interesting graphic art appears in movies. For instance, artists Miraphora Mina and Eduardo Lima were responsible for all of the graphic art in the Harry Potter movies. Over a ten-year period, they designed all of the posters, letters, newspapers, invitations, and book covers that appear in the films.

For example, since Hogwarts School of Witchcraft and Wizardry has a Gothic, almost medieval look, all written notices that come out of the school look the same way—from the style of print to the paper on which they are printed. And for official decrees from the Ministry of Magic, Mina and Lima decided on a cleaner, more modern style of graphics. The seamy, unpleasant personality of reporter Rita Skeeter is reflected in what the artists call a "gaudy and salacious" book cover they designed for Skeeter's tell-all book about Professor Dumbledore. The artists also enjoyed creating the signs and packaging in Weasleys' Wizard Wheezes shop in the style that two teenaged boys might choose.

Much of their work is relegated to the background in the movies and sometimes is not even clearly visible to viewers. One example is a sky-blue poster advertising the 422nd Annual Quidditch Tournament—an event that was part of the third movie. That poster and many other graphic designs are displayed at the Wizarding World of Harry Potter theme park in Orlando, Florida, where audiences can view—and even purchase—copies.

Quoted in Sammy Medina, "Meet the Duo Behind the Graphic Design Wizardry of 'Harry Potter,'" *Fast Company*, July 3, 2013. www.fastcodesign.com.

say, but how they look. The car's front bumper appears to have crashed into the paragraphs, scattering and damaging the words themselves.

In other instances the type style can be effective in expressing a mood. When publishers at Scholastic, an American company, decided to the print an American version of the popular Harry Potter books by British author J.K. Rowling, they made significant changes to the graphic art of the originals. Besides having a different artist do the illustrations for the books, designers chose a strikingly different font to create the cover logo. Done in what has come to be called the Harry Potter font, the title is made up of long, spiky letters. The most interesting is the capital *P*, which has a tail that ends in a lightning bolt—a nod to Harry's famous scar.

The combination of printing processes, type fonts, and creative talent in illustration and photography has provided the tools for graphic art. Even more exciting, however, are the thousands of ways that graphic artists have found to employ those tools.

Chapter Two

The Art of the Poster

One popular kind of graphic art is the poster. Long before radio, television, and the Internet, people all over the world depended on posters as a means of advertising their services or products or promoting an upcoming event such as a concert or an auction. In the United States in the early nineteenth century, posters offered rewards for lost property—from a pair of eyeglasses to a runaway slave. One poster commissioned and distributed by the US Department of War in April 1865 offered a $100,000 reward leading to the capture of John Wilkes Booth for the murder of President Abraham Lincoln.

Unlike books or pamphlets, posters were sparsely written so that the information would be clear and easy for a passerby to absorb. Many cities and towns had a public square where posters could be displayed. These early posters were called broadsides, meaning that they were printed on one side of an oversized sheet of paper. These broadsides were considered ephemera, intended not to be permanent but rather to have an immediate impact and then be thrown away—much like the posters found tacked to telephone poles or bulletin boards in the twenty-first century.

The Birth of Lithography

Since broadsides were meant to attract attention, printers developed many new typefaces that were both larger and fancier than the types used for other jobs. Because of the expense and weight of the larger type, many of these new typefaces were done with etched wood, rather than metal. Wooden blocks could also be carved to provide illustrations for the poster, although this task was often both expensive and time-consuming.

The most crucial advance in poster making was the invention of a process called lithography (meaning "stone printing" in Greek). Lithography was based on the chemical principle that oil and water do not mix. In 1796 a German actor and playwright named Alois Senefelder was looking for an inexpensive way to publish the plays that he wrote. Unable to afford the high cost of printing on engraved metal printing plates, he stumbled upon the idea of using stones as plates.

Senefelder's method involved writing with a grease pencil on a limestone tablet, after which he applied water to the stone. Because the grease pencil was oil based, the water moistened every part of the stone's surface except where the writing was. Senefelder then applied an oil-based ink to the stone, which adhered only to the writing since the stone was wet. After placing a sheet of paper over the stone and going over it with a roller, Senefelder found that the ink transferred easily to the paper.

> **Words in Context**
> *broadside*
> Early posters printed on one broad (oversized) piece of paper.

The new process had one disadvantage, however, in that the image had to be drawn in reverse; otherwise, the printed image would come out backward. On the other hand, one important advantage of lithography was that printers no longer needed to rely constantly on the same fonts and typefaces. In addition, lithography eliminated the expense of having metal type made or wooden blocks carved for illustrations. And because the letters were hand drawn—in whatever size or style the poster maker chose—there were virtually no limits to what the artist could do.

Printing in Color

Senefelder soon began experimenting with using color for his posters. He discovered that by using three different stones—each with the ink

Lithography and Offset Printing

Lithographic printing, developed in 1796, is still in use today but with modern adaptations. One common lithographic technique, offset printing, is used for books, newspapers, magazines, and brochures. This technique allows an inked image to be transferred (or offset) from a printing plate to a rubber blanketed cylinder and then to a printing surface such as paper. During the offset printing process, water and ink are applied to a chemically treated plate cylinder. When an image is transferred to the cylinder, the chemicals cause the image to accept the ink and reject the water. At the same time, blank spaces reject the ink. The inked image is transferred from the plate cylinder to the blanket cylinder, which then transfers the image to paper.

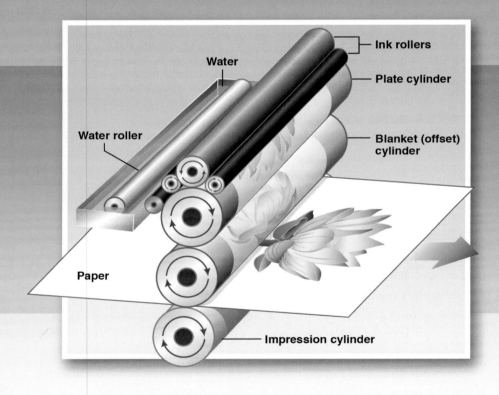

Source: Offset Printing Technology, "Offset Lithography," 2014. www.offsetprintingtechnology.com.

of one of the three primary colors blue, red, and yellow—he was able to print in virtually any color as the inks blended. He soon realized that the possibilities of lithography were endless, and he predicted that the process would be used to print and circulate not only black-and-white posters composed of text, but also colorful works of art. Senefelder wrote: "I have obtained the handsomest and darkest green by printing the design blue first and then printing it over a yellow plate, so that the yellow lay over the blue. . . . This printing with various colors is a process for which the stone is superior, and it is susceptible of such perfection that in future true paintings will be produced by its means."[9]

Graphic artists were quick to experiment with Senefelder's methods, and the use of lithography expanded rapidly. By the 1840s many designers were using his process as an inexpensive and quick means of printing maps, portraits, and diagrams on posters as well as in books. In 1843 a London entrepreneur named Henry Cole used lithography to create the world's first commercially produced Christmas card.

But it was posters whose status grew the most by means of lithography. Not only could they be made more colorful than the posters of the past, but they could be made bigger. Lithography enabled printers to produce posters that were 32 inches by 46 inches (81 cm by 117 cm)—nearly ten times as large as the ones made on regular printing presses. Because of their color and increased size, posters were capable of communicating in ways that had not been done before. For example, a poster advertising the coming of a circus could show ringmasters, lions, fierce tigers, and seals playing musical instruments all in color and be so large that it could be viewed from a greater distance than the earlier, small black-and-white posters.

> **Words in Context**
> *lithography*
> A method of printing from a flat surface (such as a smooth stone or metal plate) that has been prepared so that the ink will only stick to the design to be printed.

The Posters of Chéret

In the 1860s a Parisian printer's apprentice and artist named Jules Chéret began perfecting what Senefelder had begun, taking color and design to an entirely new level and transforming the poster into a brand-new art form. As Chéret became more familiar with the process of lithography, he began to understand the possibilities of combining it with art.

Chéret spent hours drawing on lithographic stones, using bright, vivid colors of oil-based ink or paint to make his art more exciting. He wanted not only the printed image to be visible, but the background color, too—just as it would be in a painting. Many of his posters had a beige or light blue background. Over these backgrounds he added characters—often young women dancing—wearing reds, blacks, and yellows. Sometimes he created an even more striking effect by using black as the background.

Chéret's work caused an immediate sensation. One reason was the subject matter; the young women were happy and confident, showing Paris as a vibrant, joyous city. The eye-popping color was exciting, too—unlike any posters the public had seen before. The public began referring to the women in the posters as Cherettes and eagerly awaited every new poster. In addition, people enjoyed Chéret's experiments with the size of his work. Occasionally his posters—sometimes printed in segments—were an astonishing 8 feet (2.5 m) tall!

Another contributing factor to the popularity of Chéret's work and that of other French poster makers he inspired was that the posters were easily accessible to the public. A law passed in France in 1881 lifted many censorship restrictions, allowing posters to be displayed anywhere except on churches or in areas that were designated for official notices. The lifting of these restrictions, says designer Philip B. Meggs, almost immediately led to a poster boom: "The streets became an art gallery for the nation, as even the poorest worker saw the environment transformed by images and color. Respected painters felt no shame at creating advertising posters. [There was] a new respect for the applied arts [such as advertising] and Jules Chéret showed the way."[10]

Posters Go to War

The carefree, celebratory mood of the Paris posters gave way to another style of poster, however, when World War I began in Europe

This poster advertising lamp oil was created in 1891 by French artist Jules Chéret, whose works depicting vibrant, carefree young women became wildly popular, each new one eagerly anticipated by the public.

in 1914. France, Russia, and Britain—known as the Allied forces—joined to fight Germany and Austria-Hungary. The United States entered the war on the side of the Allied forces in April 1917. Because of the sheer scope of the war, with 15 million combatants and civilians killed, it became known as the Great War.

The Posters of Ester Hernandez

Born in 1944 Ester Hernandez is a graphic artist who grew up in a California migrant farmworker community. Through her art, she became one of the most creative protesters against the foul conditions endured by the farmworkers.

One of her most famous works is a poster known as *Sun Mad*, a protest against the poisonous chemicals and pesticides to which farmworkers are exposed when picking grapes for the Sun-Maid raisin company. At first glance, her poster looks like the familiar red-and-yellow Sun-Maid raisin box, but a second look reveals something more sinister. Instead of the pretty, dark-haired woman holding a large basket of grapes is a skeleton with a red bonnet. Hernandez also changed the name of the raisins to "Sun Mad." The words "Unnaturally grown with insecticides, miticides [used to kill mites], herbicides, fungicides" appear at the bottom.

She recalled later how she used art as a way of communicating her anger. "I focused on something personal," she says. "Slowly I began to realize how to transform the Sun Maid and unmask the truth behind the wholesome figures of agribusiness. *Sun Mad* evolved out of my anger and my fear of what would happen to my family, my community, and to myself." Since the 1960s Hernandez's art has shone a spotlight on issues of poverty, civil rights, and the environment as they relate to agribusiness. She currently teaches at California State University–Los Angeles in the Chicano Studies Department.

Quoted in Smithsonian American Art Museum, "Ester Hernandez." http://american art.si.edu.

Quoted in Therese Thau Heyman, *Posters American Style*. New York: National Museum of American Art, Smithsonian Institution in association with H.N. Abrams, 1998, p. 123.

This was the first war in which posters played a key role. One important aim of the poster was to increase recruitment. In Britain, for example, there was no conscription, or draft, so many posters addressed the desperate need for more soldiers. British artists produced scores of posters urging men to enlist. Some appealed to a sense of patriotism, showing beautiful images of England and happy families—reminding enlistees what they would be fighting for. Other artists took a different approach, shaming any able-bodied man who decided not to enlist. One of these, by artist Savile Lumley, shows a little girl sitting on her father's lap asking, "Daddy, what did YOU do in the Great War?"[11] The man—clearly not a veteran by the stricken, uncomfortable look on his face—looks away, considering how to answer.

One of the eeriest images—and one of the most effective—was a poster created by American artist Fred Spear after a German submarine torpedoed the *Lusitania*, a British passenger liner, on May 7, 1915. Nearly twelve hundred people—ninety-four of them children—were killed. Spear's art shows a lovely woman, presumably a *Lusitania* passenger, submerged in the ocean with her baby in her arms. The only word on the poster is "ENLIST." The art's message was clear—unless men joined the fight, the Germans would continue to commit similar horrible acts against innocent civilians. Poster historian Maurice Rickards cites Spear's poster as "perhaps the most powerful of all war posters."[12]

Loose Lips Sink Ships

War posters have not been limited to encouraging enlistment. In June 1942, after the outbreak of World War II, the US Office of War Information (OWI) was created to be a conduit between the military and civilians. One of the OWI's primary jobs was to recruit painters, illustrators, and designers to produce posters that would generate support for the war as well as inform civilians about ways they could assist the war effort.

One of the key themes of these new posters was that enemies of the United States could be anywhere, listening in on conversations. Many wartime posters warned family members of soldiers and sailors to be careful not to talk openly about where their loved ones were stationed. One sinister poster commissioned by the OWI shows a man's hand wearing a swastika insignia ring and putting pieces of a map puzzle together. The text reminds the viewer, "Bits of careless talk are pieced together by the enemy."[13] But the most commonly used text on such posters was the phrase "Loose Lips Might Sink Ships,"[14] accompanied by art showing a burning ship sinking. The phrase grew in use and importance, appearing constantly not only in war posters but also in newspaper articles, radio broadcasts, and even public service announcements that ran in movie theaters before the main feature began.

Some famous posters were aimed at military personnel—reminding them that when they were home on leave, they too should avoid "loose lips." Posters reminded soldiers or sailors entering a battle zone not to write home with any information about their future assignments. One poster that was displayed on many American military bases shows a helmeted soldier with a zipper where his mouth should be. Another shows a drowning sailor with his torpedoed ship sinking in the background. The text says simply, "Someone talked."[15]

The Importance of Civilians

Some of the most positive posters were aimed at the home front and reminded civilians that their support was valuable to the war effort. For example, in the United States women filled a key role. With so many men enlisting, many of the factories and munitions plants began hiring women for jobs traditionally done by men. In fact, from 1940 to 1944 the number of American women in the workforce increased from 12 million to 20 million.

One of the most famous posters features a woman who became the symbol of the changing workforce. In 1942 the Westinghouse Company commissioned an artist named J. Howard Miller to create a series of posters to boost morale for the war effort. The most famous of the series shows a young woman worker flexing her biceps. The text above the art says, "We Can Do It!"[16]

In 1943 illustrator Norman Rockwell gave that woman a name. In a cover painted for the *Saturday Evening Post*, he showed a woman on a lunch break with a riveting gun on her lap. Her feet rest on a copy of Adolf Hitler's book, *Mein Kampf*—blatantly showing disdain for the German leader—and her lunch pail is labeled "Rosie." The Westinghouse poster and Rockwell's popular cover spawned a song called "Rosie the Riveter" in the 1940s, and decades later Rosie became a symbol used in the women's movement.

Psychedelic Art and Posters

Twenty-five years after the end of World War II, posters reflected a different sort of attitude—as well as a style of graphic design known as psychedelic art. This art was based on the experience of some artists and designers who tried hallucinogenic drugs such as mescaline and LSD. The images could be anything from rock stars to mushroom clouds, but poster makers' use of color and strange, difficult-to-read lettering made them easily identifiable as psychedelic art.

The color combinations of psychedelic art posters were unusual—glaring pinks, oranges, and reds together, or bright blues and greens in

Artist Wes Wilson stands in front of posters he created in the style known as psychedelic art. The text in works using this style is often difficult to read, distorted to fit into the shapes of images.

checkered or swirling patterns. The text of the posters was meant to be difficult to read, often written in puffy block letters that were bent into shapes to fit the images on the poster. Early psychedelic poster makers insisted that the only way to read the poster text was to be under the influence of psychedelic drugs. New Yorker Jeff Reid, now in his sixties, remembers how prolific such posters were during his university days:

> I was a sophomore in 1969, and you couldn't find a room in the dorm that didn't have a [psychedelic] poster. The connotation wasn't necessarily that you were using drugs. But it did show that you were supportive of the hippie thing—peace and love, and very much against the war [in Vietnam]. My roommate had a poster that showed [President Richard] Nixon in psychedelic colors, pink and orange, and he was waving a flag with the peace symbol.[17]

Posters and Protests

Through the years many artists and designers have used their talents to create posters as a medium for public protest. Some used art and text to shock, whereas others adopted a nonconfrontational tone.

One nonconfrontational antiwar poster was popular during the Vietnam War. Created in 1967 by Lorraine Schneider, the poster features a drawing of a sunflower. The drawing is childlike, as is the lettering, which reads, "War is not healthy for children and other living things."[18] Because of the tone of the statement and the simple drawing, the poster offered an antiwar message that was impossible to contradict, no matter what one believed about the politics of the Vietnam War.

Some posters depend on irony to get their message across. Poster makers often tinker with a well-known image to produce a completely new message. For example, one poster protested the war in Iraq by using then president George W. Bush's face as the familiar Uncle Sam

America's Uncle Sam

One of the most recognized images in the United States is that of Uncle Sam, whose stern face appeared on recruitment posters for both World War I and II. Uncle Sam was the creation of New York artist James Montgomery Flagg, who began selling his illustrations to magazines at age twelve. As his talent developed he became a contributing illustrator for magazines such as *Collier's Weekly, Ladies' Home Journal*, and the *Saturday Evening Post*. In 1917 he was asked to be part of the US government's Committee of Pictorial Publicity to publicize the need for civilian support during World War I. During that war, he created forty-six posters, the most famous of which featured the image of Uncle Sam, a bearded man dressed in red, white, and blue, pointing directly at the viewer and saying, "I Want YOU for the U.S. Army."

During World War II Flagg presented President Franklin D. Roosevelt with a copy of the poster and confided to the president that he saved money on modeling fees by using himself as the model for Uncle Sam. Impressed, Roosevelt responded: "I congratulate you on your resourcefulness in saving model hire. Your method suggests Yankee forebears."

Flagg's image of Uncle Sam has been used in modern times, too. In one case an Uncle Sam poster with New York City mayor Rudy Giuliani's face was used to ask for aid after the September 11, 2001, terrorist attack on the World Trade Center.

Quoted in American Treasures of the Library of Congress, "The Most Famous Poster," July 27, 2010. www.loc.gov.

symbol for the United States. Instead of the usual "I Want You!" however, this Uncle Sam says, "I Want YOUR BLOOD for Oil."[19] Another poster pictures the traditional Uncle Sam bandaged, bruised, and hatless. Instead of "I Want You!" the text proclaims, "I Want Out!"[20]

An innovative environmental poster by graphic artist Paula Scher urges viewers to reduce their energy consumption. The poster features a close-up image of a red electrical cord, and the text reads, "Unplug the little devil."[21] Scher explained later that she was struck by the fact that plugs have prongs that look very much like horns—making it an easy visual comparison.

The medium of the poster has played many important roles in society—from the simple communication of upcoming events to expressing anger or dissatisfaction with government officials to helping a nation fight a war. In the twenty-first century, posters have a role to play, too—especially in large urban environments. "If posters were not an available medium," notes Planetizen, a public interest urban exchange site, "it is probably fair to say that it would mean the loss of an essential component of participatory civic life."[22]

Chapter Three

The Art of Selling

Graphic art is a mainstay of advertising. Whether designing a print ad for a newspaper or magazine or a colorful package for a new product, graphic artists play a key role in making the product attractive and interesting. One of the first steps for a company with a new service or product is to hire graphic artists to design an image that can best represent it.

The Logo

Designing a logo is a huge part of an advertising campaign. A logo is the symbol of the product or company, an image or design that a consumer can identify quickly. A hungry driver who sees a logo showing two yellow arches does not require text to understand that a McDonald's restaurant is near. A hood ornament consisting of a circle divided into thirds on a luxury car lets one know at a glance the car is a Mercedes-Benz. On a laptop computer, a glowing image of an apple with a bite taken out of it identifies the machine as a product of Apple. And that white swoosh symbol on a pair of sneakers means that they are made by Nike.

Companies invest large amounts of money—often millions of dollars—for a logo design that will represent them on the products they sell, the building or factory from which they work, and even the stationery they use. Marketer Greg Cohen explains:

> It's not just a random design. The artist doing a logo needs to know what the company wants its image to be, how they want to be seen by consumers. Sometimes that involves surveys or market research groups to talk with consumers

and see what kinds of feelings they have about a certain logo or design. Does it make them more interested in trying that product? Is it friendly? Or does it convey something else? All that information helps the artist later on when he or she is creating a logo. You want the consumer to see the logo and instantly understand who makes that product. Quite often the most successful logos are the ones that need no lettering at all.[23]

Sometimes It Is the Text

Though most logos involve an image or design along with some text, a few highly successful logos consist of text alone. One that is frequently mentioned by graphic artists is that of Coca-Cola. The beverage was created by John S. Pemberton in 1885. He intended it as a medicinal drink and named it Coca-Cola after its two "medicinal" ingredients—coca leaves and kola nuts. (Cocaine was commonly used at the time to settle stomachs and relieve pain and would not be banned until 1914.) Pemberton wanted the original name to be Coca-Kola, but product developers convinced him that a double capital *C* in the name would be more attractive to the eye.

The logo for the new drink was simply the name "Coca-Cola" written in a black script known as Spencerian, with elongated tails on the first *C* in "Coca" and the *C* in "Cola." By the beginning of the twentieth century, the name was written in red script on a white background. In the 1940s graphic artists reversed the colors, using white letters on a red background. Since then the logo has not changed significantly, and throughout the world—no matter what language the words are written in—the logo needs no art. Interestingly, coca leaves are still used as a flavoring in the beverage, though only after a pharmaceutical company has extracted all cocaine from them.

Logos Evolve

Although Coca-Cola's logo has changed little over the decades, other successful logos have evolved to keep up with the times. For example,

The golden arches of the McDonald's restaurant chain comprise one of the most recognized corporate logos in the world.

in 1971 a new coffee company was trying to decide on a name and logo for its stores. Because the company was located in Seattle, its leaders wanted a nautical theme. They toyed with calling the business Pequod's, after the name of the whaling ship in Herman Melville's classic novel *Moby-Dick*, but the company's founders did not like the name. They finally decided on Starbucks, after Starbuck, the name of the chief mate on the *Pequod*.

The image in the Starbucks logo—appearing on its white coffee cups, packaged coffee, and store signs—has been incorrectly identified as a mermaid. She is actually a mythological creature called a siren. In ancient stories sirens were beautiful sea nymphs who could lure unwary sailors into wrecking their ships on the rocks with their eerie, haunting songs—perhaps an appropriate logo for those who cannot resist their morning coffee.

Starbucks' logo began as a small, circular brown image of the siren with a forked tail, surrounded by the text "Starbucks Coffee • Tea • Spices."[24] Eventually, the brown was changed to green, and the art showed only the siren's face. For the company's fortieth anniversary

The logo for Coca-Cola is so distinctive that it is easily recognized even when the words are written in a language besides English. The words on the bottle shown at right are in Arabic.

in 2011, Starbucks eliminated the text completely, including the Starbucks name. Company officials believed that the siren's face had made the transition to icon, the term for a logo that is so effective that it is recognizable to all without identifying the company it represents by name.

"Like Someone's Face"

Logo changes like Starbucks' sometimes result in unexpected backlashes. Graphic artists and marketing experts have learned that in many cases, consumers tend to develop a fondness for a particular logo. "A logo is almost like someone's face," says Laura Oswald, a Chicago market research company director. "If they change it, it's almost like you don't recognize the person anymore."[25]

In the case of Starbucks, the company received comments critical of its 2011 logo change. In fact, at first the negative comments on the company's Facebook page outnumbered positive comments ten to one. "We go to Starbucks for comfort, for that sense of familiarity, routine, of 'coming home,'" one customer wrote. "You've taken too much of that away with the new logo. It leaves a sour taste in my mouth more than any bitter latte ever can."[26] However, many customers felt the modernized version was acceptable, and Starbucks stuck with its revamped logo.

The Gap clothing store encountered a far more heated reaction when it changed its twenty-year-old logo consisting of a blue box in which thin white letters spell out "GAP." Graphic artists had designed a new logo in a more modern design. As one company spokesperson explained, the new logo was supposed to show the company's transition from "classic, American design to modern, sexy, cool."[27] However, within hours of the change, customers began complaining via social media as well as by calling the company's switchboard.

"This is the worst idea Gap has ever had," posted one customer on Facebook. "I will be sad to see this change take place. If this logo is brought into the clothing [store] I will no longer be shopping with the Gap. Really a bummer because 90% of my clothing has been purchased there in the last 15+ years."[28]

The corporation soon bowed to the pressure. "We've learned the hard way just how much energy there is around our brand," the company announced, "and after much thought, we've decided to go back to our iconic blue box logo."[29]

> **Words in Context**
> *icon*
> An image or logo that has become so recognizable that it no longer needs to include the name of the product it represents.

The Art of Packaging

Graphic art plays a key role in the packaging of a company's products as well as its advertising and corporate identity. Though the main function of a package is to contain and protect the product, marketing experts know that an attractive, well-designed package often is the deciding factor when a consumer chooses one product over another. Notes marketing expert Sam Ashe-Edmunds:

> The graphics on your packaging can convey messages or evoke feelings in consumers, based on the images and colors you use. Different shades of blue are considered cool, relaxing colors, while reds, oranges and yellows are seen as hot or exciting. Children respond to cartoons and drawings. Photos of people using your product can create empathy or reassurance.[30]

Many companies hire graphic artists to design eye-catching packages that will persuade a customer to try their products. For example, the Festina watch company, which has prided itself on its elegant wristwatches since 1902, wanted to demonstrate the durability of its diver's watches. In 2011 Festina began packaging its watches in clear plastic bags filled with water. The graphic artist decided that the watch in water served as the art for the packaging, making text on the bag, other than the company logo and slogan, unnecessary. It was, according to one expert, "a striking and convincing packaging solution . . . [that] demonstrates the advantage of the watch without the need for words."[31]

Newer companies as well as long-established ones like Festina can benefit from artistic packaging. For example, a company that makes strawberry, kiwi, and banana juice boxes wanted to show how fresh its juices were. Famed Japanese graphic artist Naoto Fukasawa created boxes whose surfaces look astonishingly like the fruits from which the juices are made. "I imagined that if the surface of the package imitated the colour and texture of the fruit skin," he explains, "then the object would reproduce the feeling of the real skin."[32]

Graphic Art Creates a Market

In some cases packaging decisions have revolutionized a product's usefulness. One famous example is Kleenex, a brand of tissues that were originally marketed to women for removing cold cream. Many advertisements for Kleenex featured movie stars like Helen Hayes and Ronald Coleman taking off their theater makeup using the product.

Is the Trix Rabbit Looking at You?

One of the most important goals of graphic artwork involved in designing packaging is to make the product as attractive as possible to its target consumer. In the case of the cereals intended to appeal to children, this frequently includes the use of cartoon characters—recognizable as a result of the myriad television commercials that run during children's programming. Tony the Tiger, Cap'n Crunch, and the Lucky Charms leprechaun are just a few of the characters that many children recognize long before they are able to read the labels themselves.

Researchers from Cornell University's Food and Brand Lab completed a study in March 2014 aimed at learning why children fall for particular brands—even when most of them have cartoon characters on the package and when they are all on the same grocery shelf. The researchers noticed that the characters on the boxes of the most successful kids' cereals are designed so that their eyes are angled 9.67 degrees down—the perfect angle to make eye contact with a child standing in the grocery aisle.

Two boxes of the same cereal—identical except for the level at which the cartoon character's eyes are looking—were shown to children, who overwhelmingly chose the one whose eyes looked down rather than straight ahead. One researcher suggests that healthier cereal brands could get a leg up on the sugary brands by beating them at their own game. "Put Scooby-Doo on the healthy cereals," he says, "and have Scooby look right at them."

Quoted in Jessica Mador, "You're Not Dreaming. Cap'n Crunch IS Staring at You," BringMeTheNews, April 4, 2014. www.bringmethenews.com.

Two important decisions in graphic art during the 1930s changed the way Kleenex was used. First, designer and inventor Andrew Olsen found an ingenious way to package Kleenex. He developed what became known as a "pop-up serv-a-tissue," allowing a user to take a tissue without holding on to the box. As one advertisement bragged, "One of the things you will like about Kleenex tissues is the unique patented box they come in. Kleenex tissues are fed up one double sheet at a time!"[33]

The second decision created a whole new market for Kleenex. In those days there were no disposable tissues; people carried cloth handkerchiefs in case they needed to blow their nose. But graphic artists created ads that showed people with colds or flu using Kleenex instead of cloth handkerchiefs. The text of the ads insisted that Kleenex was far more sanitary than a handkerchief, because a fresh tissue was used each time—unlike a cloth handkerchief that was used over and over. "Don't Carry a Cold in Your Pocket,"[34] the ads warned. Consumers loved the idea, and the company fueled the growing sensation by offering five dollars for ideas to keep well by using Kleenex. From cleaning the mouthpiece of a public phone with a Kleenex before using it to using the tissues to dab away one's tears in a sad movie, people had embraced the ideas of the graphic artists.

Packaging Evolution

Just as logos go through changes over the life of a product, the graphic art on packaging does, too. In some cases the reason is simply to update or modernize the style of the art or the design of the package. In other cases, however, the change is necessary because the old package reflects racial or ethnic stereotyping.

One key example is the package for Cream of Wheat cereal. Until the 1920s, when the image on the package was changed to the face of Chicago chef Frank L. White, the box featured an African American waiter named Rastus (then a pejorative term for an uneducated black person). Rastus held a sign meant to be humorous at the time but that seems painfully racist and stereotypical today: "Maybe Cream of Wheat ain't got no vitamines. I don't know what them things is. If they's bugs they ain't none in Cream of Wheat but she's sho' good to eat and cheap. Cost about 1 cent fo' a great big dish." (signed) Rastus."[35]

Aunt Jemima, another packaging icon, was the image of a black woman that evoked associations with slavery. She was the embodiment of the stereotypical plump southern "mammy," wearing a rag

Until the 1980s the image of Aunt Jemima, featured on products including pancake mix, evoked associations with slavery due to her stereotypical appearance.

on her head and speaking incorrect English. In the late 1980s the company finally decided to modernize Aunt Jemima. Graphic artists removed the rag and gave her pearl earrings and a crisp white collar.

Package Change for a Bet

Some of the most interesting ideas for packaging came from designer Raymond Loewy. Loewy came up with the logos for Shell Oil, TWA, and Exxon. He also designed the Coca-Cola vending machines and even the painted design for the outside of Air Force One. But one of his most famous designs was created on a bet—improving the packaging of Lucky Strike cigarettes, also referred to as "Luckies."

"When It Rains, It Pours"

Morton Salt is the most well-known salt manufacturer in the United States. Its trademark round blue package bearing the logo of a girl with an umbrella carrying a leaking canister of salt has been around for more than a century. It is one of the few product packages that have not changed significantly in the years since its beginning, but most twenty-first-century customers are unaware of the significance of the package design.

Morton gained its advantage over other companies because it solved the eternal salt problem: Whenever it rained or even when the weather was merely humid, salt tended to clump, making it almost impossible to use. In 1911 the Morton Salt Company began adding magnesium carbonate to its salt, making it clump free whatever the weather.

The company hired an advertising agency to come up with a campaign to promote its new product. One of the ideas presented by the agency showed a little girl holding an umbrella in one hand and in the other a box of salt that was spilling out of the open spout. Sterling Morton, the secretary of the company and the son of its founder, later recalled his excitement that the graphic art would speak for itself: "Here was the whole story in a picture—the message that the salt would run in damp weather was made beautifully evident."

Quoted in Morton Salt, "History of the Umbrella Girl." www.mortonsalt.com.

Lucky Strikes were unfiltered cigarettes that came in a dark green pack with the brand name "Lucky Strike" in a red bull's-eye on the front. The package was quite distinctive, and the president of the American Tobacco Company, George Washington Hill, was so satisfied with it that he bet Loewy $50,000—the equivalent of $832,000 in 2014—that even with his amazing skill, he could not improve the cigarette package's design.

Loewy accepted the bet and made several significant changes to the package. He abandoned the green color in favor of stark white and put the Lucky Strike logo on both the front and back of the pack, instead of just the front. He insisted this would make the brand twice as likely to be noticed. He later explained: "The reverse [had been] covered with text that few people read. The green ink was expensive, had a slight smell. After—the new package is white and red target has remained unchanged. The text on the reverse has been moved to the sides, displaying the red target on both faces. Printing cost has been reduced."[36] Loewy won the bet.

The Ubiquitous Apple

Graphic art is not limited to designing advertisements, product logos, and the packages those products come in. In a few cases the graphic art that creates an identifiable symbol of a product has expanded so that even the stores selling that product reflect the graphic artist's design. The Apple computer company is the most famous example.

When Steve Jobs founded the company in 1976, his aim was to create and sell computers that were easy to use—unlike other computers that existed at the time. To reflect his aim, he chose a simple name: Apple. However, the first logo design for the company was anything but simple. Created by Ronald Wayne, one of Jobs's cofounders, the design was an intricate woodcut of a man identifiable as seventeenth-century scientist Isaac Newton. He sat under an apple tree reading, with an apple dangling over his head. The accompanying text said, "Newton . . . A Mind Forever Voyaging Through Strange Seas of Thought . . . Alone."[37]

Words in Context

woodcut
An artistic technique in which a printer carves an image into the surface of a block of wood, and then covers the raised portions with ink.

That design lasted just a year, until Jobs hired graphic designer Rob Janoff to create an uncomplicated but memorable design for Apple. The result was an apple with a bite taken out of it. "I designed it with a bite for scale, so people get that it was an apple, not a cherry,"[38] Janoff later explained.

At first the apple was multicolored, but by 1998 it had become monochromatic—white on silver computers and silver on white computers. Without a doubt, Apple's logo has become one of the most recognized throughout the world for its clean simplicity—reflecting the simplicity of the company's products.

But the sleek monochromatic style has come to define Apple stores, too. The more than four hundred stores in fifteen countries are designed to have an uncluttered look that mimics the streamlined appearance of the electronics they sell—something that is not lost on those who walk in the door. "Basically the only real color you see when you come in are the blue shirts of the people who work here," says Janice Patterson, an Apple customer who says she has been impressed by the stores' design from the beginning. "It's an amazing design they've created. The floors are stone, the walls are white, the shelves and tables are just light unpainted wood. You walk in here and you can tell in two seconds that it's an Apple store."[39]

Words in Context
monochromatic
Using one basic color.

Eye-pleasing design plays an indisputable role in the sale of goods and services. Using color, placement of text, and interesting logos, graphic art makes products more interesting and appealing to consumers.

Chapter Four

The Art of Communicating

Graphic art is frequently a key element of types of communication besides advertising. Road signs that use symbols and colors to alert drivers to changing road conditions are one example. Graphic art is used to create public service billboards and signs that convey messages from reminding people about the dangers of drinking and driving to the importance of ending child abuse. Political campaigns, too, depend on a blend of art and text to depict their candidate in a positive light.

Mr. Yuk

Most graphic art used for communication is created with adults in mind; however, some symbols are specifically aimed at very young children. One of these is Mr. Yuk, an image that appears on stickers to identify a product that may be dangerous if swallowed, such as household cleaners, prescription medications, and other potentially harmful chemicals.

The idea began with Dr. Richard Moriarty, director of the poison center at the Children's Hospital of Pittsburgh in 1971. Moriarty was looking for a way to prevent the accidental poisoning deaths of small children. He wanted a warning sticker that could be placed on a dangerous container—a symbol that a child would not only understand, but also notice right away. At the time, the skull and crossbones symbol was sometimes used, but for many children,

The image of Mr. Yuk appears on labels for potentially harmful household products and is intended to warn young children not yet able to read that the labeled product is dangerous to consume.

the association with pirates—especially in Pittsburgh, whose baseball team used that logo—was not necessarily forbidding.

Moriarty contacted a public relations firm that presented a number of colors and drawings of faces to preschoolers, including a yelling face, a sad face, and a sick face. Their goal was to find out which face would best communicate to children that the contents of the container were dangerous. They also asked the children which of a series of colors they thought would be best for the face. The consensus among the children was that a fluorescent green sick face would best get the message across.

The Pittsburgh Poison Control Center held a contest for children to create a drawing for the sticker. Wendy Brown, a fourth grader from Weirton, West Virginia, submitted the winning entry. Brown's drawing was judged as "yucky" by the young children to whom it was shown—and the name "Mr. Yuk" was born. Today Mr. Yuk's face, often with the phone number of a poison control center printed beneath, is a recognized warning symbol in many countries.

Only a Second or Two

The physically largest way of communicating a message is the billboard. Most often the billboard is aimed at drivers in high-traffic areas, such as highways and busy roads, or places where many pedestrians walk, such as bustling city intersections. When designing billboard messages, graphic artists must adhere to guidelines that do not pertain to other media.

The most important is brevity. Billboards need to get their message across quickly, especially considering that drivers put themselves and others at risk if they are distracted. The Federal Highway Administration says that anything that takes a motorist's eyes off the road for more than two seconds is a distraction that can potentially impair his or her driving. One way to ensure that a billboard conveys a message without distracting drivers is to depend on the art, rather than text. The more words there are, the longer it takes a motorist to understand the billboard.

> **Words in Context**
> *public relations*
> The management of information between the public and an agency or company.

Some of the most arresting billboards are three-dimensional, such as the large ground-level billboards created by the Australian Childhood Foundation. The idea for the billboards was to show the public that many children experience abuse simply by being ignored and neglected. Each one consists of a large white sheet of paper with a child-sized mannequin behind it. Only the mannequin's legs below the knee and the feet can be seen. The text says, "Neglected children are made to feel invisible."[40]

Occasionally, billboards are used to express gratitude or goodwill. That was the case with a large billboard created in March 2014 by the city of Rava-Ruska, a Ukrainian city near the Polish border. The billboard's message was one of thanks to the people of Poland for their support during the Ukrainians' protests against the corruption of their president in the preceding months. The art was simple—a close-up image of a handshake. One hand was painted in the colors of the Polish flag, red and white; the other in Ukraine's colors, blue and yellow. The text, written in Polish, read, "He who does not abandon us in our battle for the future is our brother."[41]

The Art of Politics

Another arena in which graphic art plays a strong role is politics. For centuries, politicians have relied on graphic artists to create campaign tools ranging from gigantic billboards to campaign buttons, T-shirts, and bumper stickers. In fact, political graphic art was a part of George Washington's inauguration ceremony. Washington and his supporters wore brass buttons that proclaimed, "G.W.—Long Live the President."[42]

The first campaign buttons to feature a photograph of the candidate appeared in 1860 during Abraham Lincoln's presidential campaign. They were not pins, but rather were sewn onto clothing. By the presidential campaign of 1916, lithography was being used to print not only political posters of Woodrow Wilson and his rival, Charles E. Hughes, but also their images directly onto metal buttons.

Over the years, campaign posters and buttons gradually moved away from relying solely on photographs of the candidate accompanied by the candidate's name. Text, in the form of snappy slogans, became just as important. Sometimes the candidate's nickname was used, as in the case of Dwight Eisenhower's presidential campaign in 1952. Eisenhower, a celebrated general in World War II, was respected and admired, but his campaign managers wanted to stress his friendliness and likeability. By using Eisenhower's nickname, Ike, they hoped to give the campaign a personal feel with buttons and posters that proclaimed, "I Like Ike."[43]

The opposite was true with Jimmy Carter, who grew up in a Georgia peanut farming community. Wanting to give Carter credibility as a serious-minded intellectual who was as savvy about international issues as local rural ones, the campaign used "Not Just Peanuts"[44] as one slogan.

The Importance of Color

Colors have been important in political ads, too, though more than 99 percent of political art is done in patriotic red, white, and blue. In 1976, however, Jimmy Carter and Walter Mondale, the Democratic candidates running against Republicans Gerald Ford and Bob Dole, broke tradition and used green and white on buttons and posters that said, "Leaders for a Change."[45] In 1968 Democrat Eugene McCarthy made his antiwar stance known with posters and buttons showing a pink, pale blue, and red striped image of a dove.

Pop artist Andy Warhol designed one of the most attention-getting posters of the 1972 presidential campaign between incumbent Richard Nixon and challenger George McGovern. Even though he was a McGovern supporter, Warhol chose to do a portrait of Nixon. The poster was done in an impressionist art style, in which color and technique are used to communicate impressions or feelings about a person, rather than realistically portraying him or her.

Warhol's image was visually striking simply because of the colors he chose.

> **Words in Context**
> *impressionist*
> A word that describes an art style that uses colors to show feelings, rather than depicting a subject realistically.

Notes art editor Jonathan Jones of the *Guardian*, "Warhol's poster image of Nixon is not even a caricature; it is a portrait, derived from a photograph, not distorting Nixon's features except through colour. Nixon's face is acidic green, colliding shockingly with an orange background."[46] The only text on the poster appears at the bottom: Vote McGovern.

The Obama Poster

One of the most iconic political images of the twenty-first century was a poster designed by graphic artist Shepard Fairey for Barack Obama's 2008 presidential campaign. Fairey's design consisted of a stencil portrait of Obama in four colors—red, light blue, dark blue, and beige. The only text was a word at the bottom of the poster—either "Hope" or "Change."

Fairey's posters were a hit. Within hours he sold 350 of them, and orders kept pouring in. Just days after the election, Fairey was excited to see his poster displayed by Obama's hometown of Chicago, accompanied by well wishes from the city: "Congratulations Chicago's Own Barack Obama, President-Elect of the United States of

The campaign poster designed by artist Shepard Fairey for Barack Obama's 2008 US presidential campaign became one of the most recognized political images of the early twenty-first century.

America." The artist admitted he was overwhelmed by its success. "I didn't predict that it would take off so strongly," he said. "[But] if you want to change what's going on around you, you have to be willing to participate."[47]

Parodying Graphic Art

Some of the most effective uses of graphic art are actually parodies—variations of a well-known design meant to convey a comical or sarcastic idea completely different from the design's original meaning.

For instance, pro-war groups in the 1960s created bumper stickers and T-shirts featuring the peace symbol accompanied by text that read, "Footprint of the American Chicken."[48] The message was that those who protested the Vietnam War and urged peace were actually too cowardly to fight.

Another example involved Republican Barry Goldwater, who ran for president in 1964 on a platform urging a more aggressive foreign policy toward the Soviet Union. Goldwater quipped, "Let's lob one [a nuclear weapon] into the men's room at the Kremlin."[49] Goldwater supporters, pleased with his tough-talking style, wore buttons showing the candidate along with the slogan "In Your Heart, You Know He's Right." Opponents who were not at all sure that Goldwater had been joking about using nuclear weapons against the Soviets, however, parodied the Republican button. Theirs had a similar picture of Goldwater, but the text read, "In Your Guts, You Know He's Nuts."[50]

Some of more recent parodies have used Fairey's famous *Hope* poster of Barack Obama. One had an image of Sarah Palin, who was John McCain's running mate against Obama in 2008, with the same color scheme as the original. In fact, everything looked the same, except for one letter. Instead of "Hope," the word underneath Palin's image was "Nope."

Interestingly, the Fairey poster was used in 2013 against Obama himself. After it was revealed that the National Security Agency had

Gerald Herbert Holtom, the Creator of the Peace Symbol

One of the most enduring examples of graphic art with a political message is the peace symbol, designed by Gerald Herbert Holtom, a British graphic artist. Holtom was born in 1914 and graduated from London's Royal College of Art. When World War II began, he registered as a conscientious objector because of his strong pacifist beliefs and worked during the war years on a farm in England.

In 1958 Holtom, who opposed the proliferation of nuclear weapons, created a symbol for an organization called the Campaign for Nuclear Disarmament, or CND. His design actually shows the positions of two letters, *N* and *D* for "nuclear disarmament," in the navy's semaphore system—a system of communication used by sailors when sending information by flag signals, such as from ship to ship. In the semaphore system, the *N* is formed by a person holding a flag in each hand and pointing them toward the ground at 45 degree angles. The *D* is formed by holding one flag straight down and one straight up. Holtom overlaid lines symbolizing each flag position and then drew a circle around them—and the result came to be recognized around the world as the peace symbol. In the late 1960s and early 1970s, millions of young people sported T-shirts, tank tops, and hats displaying the peace symbol, often in tie-dyed designs, as a way to protest the war in Vietnam.

been gathering private citizens' phone and online data in an effort to counteract terrorism, several versions of the iconic poster appeared on the Internet. One parody shows the president wearing headphones. Above that image, the text reads, "Yes We Scan," a play on Obama's campaign slogan "Yes We Can," and in smaller letters underneath, "Deal With It."[51]

Asked if he resented the changes to his original design, Fairey replied: "I have never been an unconditional Obama supporter or cheerleader. So I'm pleased to see people subvert my Obama images as a way to critique him and demonstrate the wide gap between some of his promises and actions."[52]

Personal Expression

Political preferences are only one aspect of an individual's personality that can be expressed by graphic art. Many people enjoy wearing T-shirts, caps, or sweatshirts emblazoned with the logo of a sports team, a college or university, or even a favorite rock band. Dylan Keene, a Minnesota teen, saw Lady Gaga in concert and afterward ordered a shirt emblazoned with the title of her latest album. "I'd never seen Lady Gaga other than on TV," Keene says. "She was even more amazing than I had anticipated. I don't really get into band T-shirts like some people do, but the next day I ordered a Born This Way shirt online. It just brings back the whole experience—I love the feeling. I'll keep it forever."[53]

Many fans of teams feel the same way about the logos on their T-shirts. It was in the early 1960s that T-shirts became a vehicle of self-expression. From T-shirts proclaiming one's taste in music or one's loyalty to a favorite baseball team, to more sensitive revelations such as one's views on same-sex marriage or the use of animals in laboratory testing, graphic art is a mainstay in communicating those feelings.

The Art of Surviving

One of the newest trends in wearable graphic art is the creation of T-shirts aimed at consumers who have survived a life-changing event. This happened in 2005 after terrorists set off bombs on the London Transit network on July 7 and again two weeks later, on July 21. All together, fifty-three people were killed and many more injured. City officials worried that customers of the city's transit system would stop using public transportation out of fear that additional bombings would occur.

Instead, however, a sense of solidarity and defiance emerged within the city's population—not only among regular users of the transit system, but also among Londoners in general, who vowed not to be intimidated by terrorist attacks. To celebrate that spirit, graphic artists designed a T-shirt with the familiar red-and-blue London Underground logo and the phrase "Still Not Scared" printed underneath. "It was a way to show solidarity," says Evan Hollis, who still counts his T-shirt as one of his most prized possessions. "I wore it with pride back then, just like a lot of others did. [The shirt] is faded and pretty threadbare now, but it's something I'll hang on to, just to show my grandkids someday."[54]

T-shirts are often commissioned and sold in the wake of a tragedy to raise money for survivors. The 2012 shooting at Sandy Hook Elementary School in Newtown, Connecticut, which resulted in the death of twenty children and six adults, was one such tragedy. Soon afterward, the community had a T-shirt designed to raise money for the Sandy Hook Support Fund to help students and parents deal with the aftermath of the shooting. The design showed twenty children and six adults in a circle, holding hands. The art did not attempt to realistically depict any of the victims; instead, the artist used colorful childlike art, showing each smiling figure with angel wings and a first name written above. The text within the circle says simply, "Angels Among Us."

Beyond the Pink Ribbon

One growing market for wearable graphic art consists of breast cancer survivors. A generation ago women were reluctant to talk about their experience with the disease. Many would never have imagined speaking openly about it, let alone wearing an item announcing it.

That began to change in 1991, when the familiar pink ribbon that today symbolizes breast cancer awareness was first used. That year, the Susan G. Komen Breast Cancer Foundation distributed pink ribbons to participants in a New York race to raise money for survivors

Contentious Team Logos

Team logos are meant to provide an image to emblazon T-shirts and other apparel to allow fans to show their support. However, some team logos, such as those of the Washington Redskins and the Cleveland Indians, have been soundly criticized as offensive. These caricatural images of Native Americans, says the National Congress of American Indians (NCAI), are promoting a form of racism.

The team name "Washington Redskins" underneath the image of a Native American warrior is especially offensive, says Jefferson Keel of the NCAI, because of the historical origin of the term *redskin*. "[That name] originated in the bounty paid for Native body parts and human flesh," he says. "It does not honor Native people in any way, and has no place in modern American society."

To make the point that team names and logos that feature stereotypical depictions of Native Americans is wrong, the NCAI published a poster showing two baseball caps, one with a cartoonish image of a Jewish man and the other with a similar image of a Chinese man, alongside a cap bearing the logo of the Cleveland Indians. The text of the poster reads, "No race, creed, or religion should endure the ridicule faced by the Native Americans today. Please help us put an end to this mockery and racism by visiting www.ncai.org."

Quoted in Regina F. Graham, "Racism of Sports Logos Put into Context by American Indian Group," CBS Cleveland, October 8, 2013. http://cleveland.cbslocal.com.

of breast cancer. Since that time, not only the pink ribbon but also the color pink in general has become synonymous with breast cancer awareness. In October, designated as Breast Cancer Awareness Month, pink is everywhere. Companies sell everything from pink

First used in 1991 to symbolize breast cancer awareness, the pink ribbon adorns many items during Breast Cancer Awareness Month in October, including NFL gear.

M&M's candies and Tic Tac mints to pink kitchen mixers, and many NFL players wear pink shoes, gloves, caps, and wristbands to show their support.

As a result of this newfound openness, today speaking freely about cancer can take the form of buying a T-shirt with graphic art announcing that the wearer is a survivor and is not shy about it. Elaine, a fifty-eight-year-old survivor, says that she bought two T-shirts for herself after her recent mastectomy. One has the pink ribbon on it and the words "You're Looking at a Survivor," and the other one reads, "Chemo Warrior."

Elaine says she was influenced by a conversation with a nurse in the hospital, who told her that in previous decades breast cancer was viewed as a tragedy and the women who got it were looked at as victims. Elaine says:

> But today's different. It's a new world out there. I think it's healthy to be optimistic and open about things that are scary. There are a lot of reasons for hope—that's why I bought these shirts. I'm not hiding it. I'm not just some victim. This shirt I'm wearing today makes me feel good, and it lets people know I was sick but the doctors caught it in time and now I'm well. That a good reason to celebrate.[55]

Chapter Five

Graphic Arts in the Digital Age

Graphic arts underwent a tremendous amount of change in the latter half of the twentieth century. Up until then, the process of creating advertisements, political announcements, posters, and other types of visual communication was done largely as it had been for generations. The process was complicated and time-consuming, especially because so many people were involved in creating a single piece of graphic art.

A Long Process

In the 1970s, for example, a business owner who wanted to run a magazine advertisement would turn to an advertising agency, where a graphic artist would sketch out an idea on paper. The finished layout usually included a headline, body text, photographs or illustrations, and the client's logo.

Some clients were satisfied with seeing a layout that showed the idea in rough form, with squiggles for body text and simple color drawings to represent the images. Other clients wanted to see every detail, as if the ad was ready to go to the printer. This was called a mock-up. Explains the website DesignM.ag, "The goal was to make the mockup look as much like the finished product as possible so that the clients could verify whether it matched the idea and message they were looking to present."[56]

Once the client approved the design, a production artist in the agency would map out the final draft of the ad, called a keyline.

This keyliner would make sure the margins were correct for the ad space and would paste on facsimiles of the photos or illustrations to be used, along with the text and headline. Typesetting was performed by a specialized vendor who set the type in the style decided on by the graphic artist.

From there the project would go to the printer, who would make a proof—a preliminary version of the ad that included the photos and illustrations. The designers would check every detail to make sure there were no mistakes or spelling errors; this process was the source of the word *proofread*. Once the designers were satisfied that the ad was error free, it would be printed.

On-Screen Graphic Art

This process changed in 1984, when Apple introduced the Macintosh computer. Using desktop applications such as PageMaker and QuarkXPress, graphic artists were able to assemble a layout on the computer screen instead of on paper. And the artist could create a digital file instead of doing a keyline for an ad or some other piece of graphic design.

Gradually, the job of setting type also shifted to the graphic artist's personal computer. The ease with which text could be typed and adjusted was astonishing. When changes needed to be made or if an error was spotted within the text or headline, the edits could be made without delay.

But one of the most exciting aspects of the increased use of computers was that they made choosing the fonts far easier. Not only did computers arrive from the factory with a selection of fonts built into their operating systems, but companies were established to create even more fonts. One of earliest of these was Emigre, a small company that designed type of widely varying styles—from fonts with a futuristic feel to letters that appear almost three-dimensional. Emigre was the first type company to design its fonts on and for the computer.

Emigre founders Rudy VanderLans and Zuzana Licko started a magazine of the same name to showcase their designs. Note graphic design experts Seymour Chwast and Steven Heller, "The

The advent of the Apple Macintosh computer in 1984 enabled artists to use graphic arts applications to lay out ads and other print materials electronically rather than on paper.

tabloid-sized quarterly defied the tenets of Modern layout much in the same way that sixties Psychedelic poster artists upended the rules of legibility—laying down rules of their own."[57]

Digital Billboards

Besides the advent of new tools, one of the most creative advances in graphic art is the digital billboard. Unlike the older paper billboards, which were created as large painted panels and then pasted in place on a large frame, digital billboards are created by computer programs and can be changed electronically. But it is not the ease with which they can be changed that makes digital billboards exciting—it is the amazing new ads that the digital medium makes possible.

In Stockholm, Sweden, for example, a company wanted to introduce a new line of hair care products in 2014. The production company that created the ad bought space for a large display ad on a digital screen next to the tracks of an underground subway platform. The ad shows an attractive young woman with long, beautiful hair. The idea was to surprise passersby by making the ad "come to life"—having the model's long hair blow around whenever a train arrived.

Workers equipped the screen with special sensors that would engage at the moment the subway train arrived. According to Stopp Family, the production company that designed the ad, this was not an easy feat, because the designers did not want the sensors to be so sensitive that they would go off whenever a person walked by the display. "We needed to build a device that could be calibrated to sense the arrival of the train and not react to passing passengers," Stopp Family explains on its website. "Using an ultrasonic sensor . . . we [then] connected our device to the screen's computer, where the film could be activated by the passing trains."[58]

The result was amazing. With the headline "Make your hair come alive,"[59] the sensors within the billboard accomplished just that for the model, who looks as surprised as the passengers watching the billboard. On its website, the company posted a short video showing not only how it accomplished the feat, but also the excited reactions of waiting passengers. "My favorite part is when the woman in the picture kind of smiles as she smoothed out her hair," says student Aisha Haji-Mumin, who saw the digital billboard on YouTube. "To me, her reaction seemed really very realistic."[60]

Reacting to the Environment

Another powerful digital billboard was put up along a New Zealand road that was the site of many fatal accidents, especially during the area's rainy season. Hoping to lower the number of accidents, a local safety organization sponsored a billboard showing a close-up photograph of a young boy's face. The text underneath said, "Rain changes everything. Please drive to the conditions."[61]

Eerily, the billboard was designed to "bleed" when it rains, making it look as though blood is dripping from the boy's nose, mouth, and eyes. Notes one marketing blogger, "If that harrowing image doesn't make people slow down, we don't know what will."[62]

Another innovative billboard depends not only on sensors but also on aeronautic surveillance technology that identifies an airplane and its flight number. British Airlines introduced these billboards in London in November 2013. Using a stark white background, the billboards show a little boy playing on the floor. However, anytime a British Airways plane flies overhead, the boy jumps up and walks the length of the billboard, pointing directly at the jet as it flies by. The text appears, identifying the plane specifically by flight number and its place of origin. "Look!" the text says. "It's flight BA475 from Barcelona!"[63] If the plane is taking off, it is identified by its destination.

Expanding the Definition of Billboard

The creation of the digital billboard is not the only change that has been made in the way billboards operate. In 2000 the definition of what a billboard is expanded when some companies began a process called vehicle wrapping. The process begins on the computer, using a cutting-edge program called Adobe Illustrator. The program allows the user to create a large, colorful design—including text—that then is printed on a special thin vinyl adhesive wrap invented by the 3M Company.

> **Words in Context**
> *vehicle wrapping*
> A method of encasing a vehicle in printed vinyl film, allowing the vehicle to be a moving billboard for a product or service.

The vinyl film is made to envelop an entire vehicle—whether it is a car, bus, truck, or train car. The film is usually designed with bright logos or other commercial images that grab the attention of motorists. On average, a wrapped vehicle driving in a busy metropolitan area can be noticed by three thousand people every hour, making it far more visible than a stationary billboard.

One of the most interesting aspects of vehicle wrapping, especially on large vehicles such as buses and trains, is that every square

"Drag Him Away"

An interactive billboard in a London train station received a great deal of attention when it was launched in April 2012. Sponsored by the National Centre for Domestic Violence (NCDV), the billboard shows a man pointing at his partner and violently yelling at her, though viewers cannot hear what he is saying. After a moment or two, a message on the screen says, "Use your phone to stop this now. Drag him away at nckv.org.uk/stop [the web address of the organization]."

Viewers can access the website and swipe their cell phone screen to move the man away from the victim to another screen. As more and more viewers become involved, he moves from screen to screen until he in the most remote screen. At that point, a message appears explaining how to report an actual act of domestic violence to the NCDV so the organization can intervene on the victim's behalf.

The goal, according to the NCDV, is to make it clear to people that they can take action when they see someone being abused. In this case the action is only a swipe on a cell phone, but the message gets through. Reactions to the billboard have been largely positive. According to the website Trendhunter, "This fantastic new campaign looks to not only educate people on the issues of domestic violence, but involve them and make them more than bystanders in the issue."

Quoted in Jennifer Gosnell, "Interactive Billboard by NCDV Allows Texters to 'Drag Him Away,'" Trendhunter, May 7, 2012. www.trendhunter.com.

inch of the vehicle is covered with the vinyl film without affecting the passengers' view. "Even the windows are covered," says Bob Pigozzi, who owned a Minneapolis vinyl wrap business that created vehicle wraps for Target and other large companies. "But the nice thing is

Graphic art techniques today enable a bus covered in vinyl wrap, like this one in New York City, to become a moving billboard.

that visibility isn't affected at all—there are perforations in the vinyl, so passengers can see just as if the wrap weren't there. The people driving by, viewing the vehicle, though, they don't see any windows at all."[64]

A Secret Message in Lenticular Printing

Another creative way of making billboards more remarkable is the use of lenticular printing, in the past used only for three-dimensional displays. The process allows a graphic artist to print two or more images on the same surface, with each being visible from a different angle. For example, since the 1940s small toys in snack boxes such as Cracker Jack looked as though the image on the toy was winking or shaking its head when a child slightly rotated the toy.

But graphic artists have figured out a new use for lenticular printing—printing two different images in the same space, each being visible from a different angle than the other. One good example was a large ad first displayed in 2013 in Spain. A child-advocacy organization wanted to address the problem of child abuse in a dramatic new way. In this version of lenticular printing, two different photographs and messages are displayed, with very startling results.

The ads are not above buildings or roadways, as many billboards are, but at ground level on street corners or in malls. An adult—anyone taller than 4 feet 4 inches (132 cm)—viewing the ad will see a close-up photograph of a little boy, with the headline, "Sometimes child abuse is only visible to the child suffering it."[65]

A child—anyone shorter than 4 feet 4 inches, usually below age ten—will see the same little boy but with bruises on his face. The message, which only the child viewer sees, says, "If somebody hurts you, phone us and we'll help you,"[66] along with the phone number for the advocacy organization. The Grey Group, the agency that created the ad, says the idea was to have a "secret message" that only the child can see, based on the idea that the child and the adult—who is perhaps the abuser—are seeing the ad at the same time.

> **Words in Context**
> *lenticular printing*
> A style of printing that shows two different views of the same object, depending on the angle at which it is viewed.

Interactive Ads

Probably the most wide-ranging trend of graphic art in the digital age is that so much of it has become interactive. More and more ads or other messages appear on websites or within cell phone apps. That means it is essential to not only have a web address for the product or service, but have one that can be accessed with the click of a computer mouse or a tap on the cell phone's screen. Amsterdam graphic artist Elliot Stewart-Franzen notes that the success of an advertisement depends on much more than how beautiful the photography or how well-written the text is. He explains:

> It's different today than it was even five years ago. Now everybody's got a cell phone, everybody's connected. Ads today are being designed for people who have instant access to the Internet. If they see an image or an idea they like, you've got to make it easy for them to take the next step to click on the link. Ads lead to websites and Facebook pages, or feature QR [Quick Response matrix] codes that let people download additional content like songs, apps or movie trailers.[67]

Green Graphic Art

Some of the twenty-first century's most exciting graphic art is being used in ads that promote products by means of environment-oriented advertisements. Some companies that have a history of being environmentally responsible want to make sure that potential customers are aware of that. On the other hand, companies that are just becoming green want to promote their efforts as well, and they are seeking ways to call attention to what they are doing for the environment.

One such advertisement is a Volkswagen commercial produced in 2014 by the Argentina-based graphics studio by the name of Plenty. The idea was to encourage their audience—in this case, Mexican consumers—to "think blue," the color that in Mexico is associated with being environmentally friendly. Plenty's designers wanted to break from the traditional car ads that emphasize the power, luxury, and speed of the automobiles, and instead concentrate on a clean, eco-responsible future.

Instead of showing the usual film footage of the car driving on an open highway or some other appealing outdoor driving scene, Plenty uses animation to depict a clean, dreamlike all-white landscape with blue trees. The only real footage in the commercial is the silver VW. The website DigitalMeetsCulture, which gathers information on trends in digital technology throughout the world, was highly impressed. "This is a beautifully designed digital ad campaign," they write. "The only question is whether consumers prefer to be seduced by the lifestyle traditional car ads depict, or if sweet, eco-friendly animations will do the trick."[68]

Another of the green graphic art ad trends in the digital age involves the creative use of environmentally friendly materials. One remarkable example was a letter that the Honda Corporation sent in 2008 to customers of its lawn and garden equipment. The paper on which the letter was printed was made from seeds. The text of the let-

Digitally Correcting Photos

The technology of the digital age has not only made it easier for graphic artists to take beautiful photographs but also for a retoucher to correct mistakes in a photograph. Not long ago a photograph of a beautiful model would have to be reshot if a flaw showed up on the proof. Brad Palm, a master retoucher, describes working on a photo that a fashion photographer has taken for an advertisement. Palm points to the close-up photo on his computer screen: "You go in tight like this, and you can see lots of little stuff that [the fashion photographer] doesn't want. You can see little scars, moles, tiny lines or imperfections. Also, the fashion photographer wants to make the mouth look more symmetrical. And he's bothered by some of those little flyaway strands of hair, too."

For retouching, Palm uses his computer, along with what is called a digitizer tablet that allows him to use a stylus to "draw" what he wants to see on the computer screen. He can add thicker eyelashes, make subtle changes to the model's lips, and also delicately remove any little imperfections on her skin. "What we're doing is fooling the eye—*trompe l'oeil*, the French call it," says Palm. "The trick is you don't want to make her so perfect she doesn't look real. Some retouchers make the mistake of kind of buffing out all the texture, but then what's left doesn't look like skin anymore. It doesn't look real."

Brad Palm, personal interview with the author, March 3, 2014, Minneapolis, MN.

ter urged readers to plant it after reading it rather than simply throwing it away. "In terms of a green message," the letter explained, "we went beyond 'Carbon Neutral' and created an idea that would ultimately remove carbon from the atmosphere."[69]

The Importance of Graphic Art

Graphic art is a necessary and vibrant part of modern life. It is difficult to imagine a world without the combination of text and art that identifies products, helps people protest an injustice, informs the public about a social problem that needs fixing, or even communicates road conditions.

Over the centuries the simple tools used by early graphic artists have evolved into amazingly precise digital instruments. The media in which these designers work have expanded as well. Illuminated manuscripts and the first books printed on presses with movable type have, in the twenty-first century, given way to sophisticated technologies such as digital billboards, made possible by computers.

Despite these changes and innovations, however, the purposes of graphic art have remained very much the same. As graphic art and design educator Sharon Helmer Poggenpohl notes, "From humble things like gum wrappers to huge things like billboards to the T-shirt you're wearing, graphic design informs, persuades, organizes, stimulates, locates, identifies, attracts attention and provides pleasure."[70] Graphic art in the hands of creative people will continue to find ways to accomplish these goals.

Source Notes

Introduction: The "Everywhere" Art

1. Richard Hollis, *Graphic Design: A Concise History*. London: Thames & Hudson, 2001, p. 223.

Chapter One: The Foundations of Graphic Arts

2. Doris Lee Anderson, personal interview with the author, March 18, 2014, St. Paul, MN.
3. Quoted in Curtis Publishing, "Norman P. Rockwell (1894–1978)." http://curtispublishing.com.
4. Quoted in Ben Cosgrove, "Behind the Picture: 'The American Way' and the Flood of '37," *Life*, 2014. http://life.time.com.
5. Quoted in Associated Press, "Stunning 360-Degree View of NY Taken from WTC Spire," SILive.com, March 6, 2014. www.silive.com.
6. Don Berg, personal interview with the author, April 11, 2014, Minneapolis, MN.
7. Robin Landa, *Graphic Design Solutions*. Albany, NY: Delmar, 2005, p. 83.
8. Quoted in Landa, *Graphic Design Solutions*, p. 85.

Chapter Two: The Art of the Poster

9. Quoted in Alois Senefelder, *The Invention of Lithography*. Project Gutenberg, 2012. www.gutenberg.org.
10. Philip B. Meggs, *A History of Graphic Design*, 3rd ed. New York: Wiley, 1998, p. 184.
11. Quoted in Hollis, *Graphic Design*, p. 33.
12. Quoted in *Femininity in Propaganda* (blog), "'Enlist' by Fred Spear," May 10, 2011. http://ahabbestad.blogspot.com.

13. Quoted in Wolfsonian, "Bits of Careless Talk Are Pieced Together by the Enemy," 2013. www.wolfsonian.org.

14. Quoted in Eyewitness to History, "Loose Lips Sink Ships." www.eyewitnesstohistory.com.

15. Quoted in American Merchant Marine at War, "World War II Posters." www.usmm.org.

16. Quoted in Therese Thau Heyman, *Posters American Style*. New York: National Museum of American Art, Smithsonian Institution in association with H.N. Abrams, 1998, p. 106.

17. Jeff Reid, telephone interview with the author, March 16, 2014.

18. Quoted in Social Design Notes, "War Is Not Healthy," February 15, 2005. http://backspace.com.

19. Quoted in Cafe Press, "I Want Your Blood for Oil." www.cafepress.com.

20. Quoted in Stacey Vanek Smith, "Propaganda Artists Give Uncle Sam a Makeover," *Christian Science Monitor*, April 4, 2003. www.csmonitor.com.

21. Quoted in Pentagram, "Little Devil by Paula Scher." http://pentagramdesign.tumblr.com.

22. Nate Berg, "The Importance of Posters in Public Life," Planetizen, July 7, 2008. www.planetizen.com.

Chapter Three: The Art of Selling

23. Greg Cohen, telephone interview with the author, April 1, 2014.

24. Quoted in Elizabeth Fuller, "Starbucks Logo Change: No Name. More Mermaid. Will It Sell More Coffee?," *Christian Science Monitor*, January 6, 2011. www.csmonitor.com.

25. Quoted in Fuller, "Starbucks Logo Change."

26. Quoted in Fuller, "Starbucks Logo Change."

27. Quoted in Julie Weiner, "New Gap Logo, Despised Symbol of Corporate Banality, Dead at One Week," *Vanity Fair*, October 12, 2010. www.vanityfair.com.

28. Quoted in Blake Ellis, "New Gap Logo Ignites Firestorm," CNNMoney, October 8, 2010. http://money.cnn.com.

29. Quoted in Weiner, "New Gap Logo, Despised Symbol of Corporate Banality, Dead at One Week."

30. Sam Ashe-Edmunds, "Packaging Effects on Marketing," *Houston Chronicle*, 2014. http://smallbusiness.chron.com.

31. Quoted in Jessica Sanchez, "Festina Watches—Divers Watch in Water Packaging," *The Dieline* (blog), June 13, 2013. www.thedieline.com.

32. Quoted in Andrew Liszewski, "Juice Boxes with Realistic Fruit Skin," *OhGizmo!* (blog), April 4, 2009. www.ohgizmo.com.

33. Quoted in Sally Edelstein, "Colds, Flu, and the History of Kleenex," *Envisioning the American Dream* (blog). http://envisioningtheamericandream.com.

34. Quoted in Edelstein, "Colds, Flu, and the History of Kleenex."

35. Quoted in *Complex*, "The 25 Most Racist Food Advertisements," October 26, 2013. www.complex.com.

36. Quoted in Hollis, *Graphic Design*, pp. 99–100.

37. Quoted in Edible Apple, "The Evolution and History of the Apple Logo," April 20, 2009. www.edibleapple.com.

38. Quoted in Ivan Raszl, "Interview with Rob Janoff, Designer of the Apple Logo," *Creativebits* (blog), August 3, 2009. http://creativebits.org.

39. Janice Patterson, personal interview with the author, March 10, 2014, Edina, MN.

Chapter Four: The Art of Communicating

40. Quoted in *Propaganda for Change* (blog), "Neglected 'Invisible' Children," February 1, 2013. http://persuasion-and-influence.blogspot.com.

41. Quoted in A.C., "Neighbours and Brothers," *Eastern Approaches* (blog), *Economist*, March 3, 2014. www.economist.com.

42. Quoted in George Washington 1789, "Isabela's 1798 George Washington Inaugural Buttons." http://georgewashingtoninauguralbuttons.com.

43. Quoted in Pamela Wiggins, "Presidential Campaign Buttons," About.com: Antiques, 2014. http://antiques.about.com.

44. Quoted in Tracy Keller, "Win or Lose: Memorable Presidential Slogans," Concordia University, November 7, 2012. http://online.csp.edu.

45. Quoted in Kathleen Hall Jamieson, *Packaging the Presidency: A History and Criticism of Presidential Campaign Advertising*. New York: Oxford University Press, 1984, p. 376.

46. Jonathan Jones, "Richard Nixon, Andy Warhol (Vote McGovern) 1972," *Guardian* (Manchester), February 10, 2001. www.theguardian.com.

47. Quoted in Laura Barton, "Hope—the Image That Is Already an American Classic," *Guardian* (Manchester), November 10, 2008. www.theguardian.com.

48. Quoted in Cecil Adams, "What's the Origin of the Peace Symbol?," Straight Dope, August 9, 1995. www.straightdope.com.

49. Quoted in PBS, "Barry Goldwater," 2005. www.pbs.org.

50. Quoted in PBS, "Barry Goldwater."

51. Quoted in Juliet Lapidos, "Yes We Can to Yes We Scan," *Taking Note* (blog), *New York Times*, July 18, 2013. http://takingnote.blogs.nytimes.com.

52. Quoted in David Ng, "Shepard Fairey Approves of NSA Parodies of His Obama 'Hope' Poster," *Los Angeles Times*, June 27, 2013. http://articles.latimes.com.

53. Dylan Keene, telephone interview with the author, April 1, 2014.

54. Evan Hollis, personal interview with the author, March 2, 2014, Minneapolis, MN.

55. Elaine, personal interview with the author, March 31, 2014, Minneapolis, MN.

Chapter Five: Graphic Arts in the Digital Age

56. DesignM.ag, "How the Mighty Computer Changed the Industry." http://designm.ag.

57. Steven Heller and Seymour Chwast, *Graphic Style: From Victorian to New Century*, 3rd ed. New York: Abrams, 2011, p. 235.

58. Quoted in Matt Blake, "This Ad Will Blow You Away!," *MailOnline*, February 28, 2014. www.dailymail.co.uk.

59. Quoted in Blake, "This Ad Will Blow You Away!"

60. Aisha Haji-Mumin, personal interview with the author, April 13, 2014, Minneapolis, MN.

61. *Creative Bloq* (blog), "30 Must-See Examples of Billboard Advertising," April 7, 2014. www.creativebloq.com.

62. *Creative Bloq* (blog), "30 Must-See Examples of Billboard Advertising."

63. Quoted in Zach Honig, "British Airways' Digital Billboard Identifies Planes as They Pass Overhead," *Engadget* (blog), November 22, 2013. www.engadget.com.

64. Bob Pigozzi, telephone interview with the author, April 11, 2014.

65. Quoted in Todd Wasserman, "Billboard Shows Different Messages for Kids and Adults," Mashable, May 6, 2013. http://mash able.com.

66. Quoted in Neetzan Zimmerman, "Child Abuse Billboard Contains 'Secret Message' Not Visible to Adults," *Gawker* (blog), May 6, 2013. http://gawker.com.

67. Elliot Stewart-Franzen, telephone interview with the author, April 14, 2014.

68. Quoted in Lucia Ruggiero, "Plenty Create an Eco-friendly World for Volkswagen," Digital Meets Culture, 2014. www.digi talmeetsculture.net.

69. Quoted in Frederik Samuel, "Honda Letter," *Advertising/Design Goodness* (blog). www.frederiksamuel.com.

70. Sharon Helmer Poggenpohl, "What Is Graphic Design?," American Institute of Graphic Arts, 1993. www.aiga.org.

For Further Research

Books

Margo Bergman, *Street Smart Advertising: How to Win the Battle of the Buzz*. Lanham, MD: Rowman & Littlefield, 2010.

Stephen J. Eskilson, *Graphic Design: A New History*. New Haven, CT: Yale University Press, 2012.

Ann Ferebee, *A History of Design from the Victorian Era to the Present*. New York: Norton, 2011.

Steven Heller and Seymour Chwast, *Graphic Style: From Victorian to New Century*. 3rd ed. New York: Abrams, 2011.

Roger Walton, ed., *The Big Book of Graphic Design*. New York: Collins Design, 2007.

Websites

American Institute of Graphic Arts (www.aiga.org). The American Institute of Graphic Arts is the oldest professional membership organization for graphic designers. Its website offers information about the skills and education needed to pursue a career in graphic design, as well as timely articles on interesting artists and the latest trends in design.

Creative Bloq (www.creativebloq.com). From three-dimensional billboards to one that shows a boy bleeding from a car accident, this blog shows some of the most creative billboards around the world.

The Dieline (www.thedieline.com). A fascinating blog created by a graphic artist specializing in packaging, with dozens of the most innovative ideas for products around the world.

Envisioning the American Dream (http://envisioningtheamerican dream.com). A colorful website presenting design in advertisements, political art, and other types of graphic art from various eras in American history—from the stories behind Kleenex to cigarettes to advertising during wartime, the information is well organized and very readable.

A Picture of Politics (http://apictureofpolitics.wordpress.com). This blog contains scores of well-presented protest posters as well as street art from the United States and around the world and includes the history behind the art.

Index

Picture Credits

Cover: Thinkstock Images

Maury Aaseng: 22

AP Images: 41, 46

© Stefano Bianchetti/Corbis: 13

© Mike Blake/Reuters/Corbis: 60

© Mathew Cavanagh/epa/Corbis: 6

© Bob Daemmrich/Corbis: 50

© Jonathan Ernst/Reuters/Corbis: 35

© Jacqui Hurst/Corbis: 17

© Walter McBride/Corbis: 64

© Colin McPherson/Corbis: 36

© Ted Streshinsky/Corbis: 29

© Swim Ink 2, LLC/Corbis: 25

© WD/Icon SMI/Corbis: 56

Ms 251, f.16r: The marriage of Adam and Eve from 'Des Proprietes De Choses', c.1415 (gold leaf, gold ink & tempera on parchment) (detail of 276966), Boucicaut Master, (fl.1390–1430) (and workshop)/Fitzwilliam Museum, University of Cambridge, UK/ Bridgeman Images: 10